Ledger Domain

Also by David Stanford Burr

AUTHOR

The Poet's Notebook: Inspiration, Techniques, and Advice on Craft

ANTHOLOGY EDITOR

The Love Poems of Lord Byron: A Romantic's Passion

The Love Poems of John Keats: In Praise of Beauty

Love Poems

Poems of American Spirit

Fun and Fancy

Visionary Poems

Christmas Poems

Ledger Domain

David Stanford Burr

The New York Quarterly Foundation, Inc.
Beacon, New York

NYQ Books™ is an imprint of The New York Quarterly Foundation, Inc.

The New York Quarterly Foundation, Inc.
P. O. Box 470
Beacon, NY 12508

www.nyq.org

First Edition

Set in New Baskerville

Layout by Raymond P. Hammond

Cover Design by Raymond P. Hammond

Cover Art: David Stanford Burr

Author Photo (Cover): ©Creighton: Courtesy of NYU Photo Bureau

Author Photo (Interior): ©Lauren Burr

Library of Congress Control Number: 2019934562

ISBN: 978-1-63045-063-2

In memory of
Helen and Horace Burr
them that authored me
and brought me to this dance

and to
Joan, half of *us,*
and our *offsprung,* Lauren,
who have kept it lively

CONTENTS

Animalia

Offsprung

Then

Littoral

Listen

I.

Again and again comes the loud flow
in between the quiet ebbing
like inhalation and exhalation
there is this snoring along the long shore
tonight, before I give into my own
roar, I subside by resting on my side,
better to listen to the larger echo,
cosmic heartbeat pounding, receding

II.

I am taking the sounding of the sea
into the depths of my inner eardrums where
the throw of flow and the ease of ebb
beat and retreat in neat complement, an
imprecise tracking of time, where any
quartz movement is granular, natural,
pulsing the phases of earth, moon, sun as has been
millennium upon millennium.

The sea is taking the sounding of me
too in its *memento mori* way where
each wave aggregates—while my hourglass
by grains reduces its store—in countdown
of my floruit's passing in unpausing
wave after wave after wave after wave

III.

The susurrus of surf sounds beyond
the screen and the slight sea salt scent
enters my nostrils by volume and weight
as wind gently rocks the cottage, rocks this
bed in the conscious moments before sleep,
which I know will be mosquito interrupted—
a small blood offering's down payment

on a bit of paradise is not so much.
I wonder if the ocean roar imprints
my dreams—not the remembered ones, those deeper—
and now I am back in her amniotic sac
swimming, breathing underwater, waiting
to gasp for air when I am slapped on the littoral
born anew into the old world made literal

Combing

Tonight I will dream of tomorrow finding
Aristotle's lantern out on the strand
that small jaw-joint from a sea urchin with
five touching tooth tips, looking
like a lighthouse lens of pyramid faces.
Not many urchins wash up here but
I will keep my beacon eye out, sweeping
swaths of beach, willing to awaken its
discovery, and to keep my eye keen I will
seek beach glass, flat stones for Go, driftwood,
whole shells, anything—especially PEACE—
so surprise at those found things will be great
even if that main finding does not betide.
Tonight I will dream of finding tomorrow.

August Spring Tide on Fire Island

The full moon rides high above scapular clouds
roils below on the quicksilver swelling
landward, its mystery whelming with shadows
and shallows in echelon, dark breaching
bar, lone greenish wave breaks pale, zippers
left and right as one long lengthening line,
the next curls, crests, plunges, crashes, swashes—
bright bubbly surf cooly sucking my toes,
backwash of moonshine and North Star.
Waves bow down one by one from their origin,
three thousand miles away, broad basaltic abyss
beneath that wind's first whipped-up ripple.

Black Spot

I walk the shore to get the ocean roar
in my inner ear where I can hear it
over the regular plodding beat
of my barefoot slap, and see its lacy
selvaging surf lap ply after ply,
lapsing back to where it begins again
to surge anew and anon—and I am
between systole/diastole of mother,
child of her great inland sea waiting to
deliver me here on the world's littoral—
as her cloud of reverie passes by
leaving me alone on this strand of beach
while a lone raven hops to carrion.

Beachhead

I cast no shadow on this littered shore,
dark spike-shaped tails sag beneath the noonday sun
as gulls fall to the smorgasbord feasted
up from the deep beyond—all morning I
have picked my way through the tumult,
shooed hook-bills off their prey, hurled
those stronger horseshoes back into the ebb—
battered, buckled by breakers, taken
by the wash.
          Too many armored warriors
dying and dead to tiptoe among—
on their shields, a beach-long hecatomb
of stilled pincers, bayonets, helmets,
mess kits, a marine armada wracked
by last night's storm.
               I reach down to
save just one living fossil—to save
myself.

We Shorebirds

The sanderlings at eventide mimic the tide's
ebb, skitter on short legs behind as it
recedes then run back or hover just above
the flow, then alight and skitter down beach,
dartle to and fro with their sharp quick-
striking bills, sucking the sand for crustaceans,
worms, mollusks, larvae. With chronic hunger,
they are brisk waders in their search of sustenance.
Back and forth they go, manic traffic, between
urgent surge and slower waning ebb.

I am a slower bird, wandering back and forth
in the intertidal zone seeking an uncertain prey
fetched up from the swell and then abandoned
as I survey, spot, scramble, and snap up—
before the flow—that measure of treasure,
meager or mighty, that I happen to snatch:
a specimen sand dollar or moon snail shell.
Regardless of success, a happy day of seeking,
mindful play of my unfocused scan of sand,
idling time in this ambling—just mine.

Then

Civil Defense

That fall the missiles seemed so near,
shadowed the kitchen's red-washed floor,
the radio shrilled and told us how
we could live through a nuclear war.

Dad's at the sink with a huge green bottle
we'd bought in Spain, too tall for the tap,
trying to fill it to take down into the earth
basement, our presto-chango bomb shelter
where the ancient oil furnace roared
and one bare lightbulb swayed on a cord.

Dad is screaming "Blankets!" "Food!"
his commands short and scared as Mom stood
poised, long red hair in a bun, smoking a Kent,
looking at him, repeating louder to his words
"If the bomb comes we will all be dead!"

Then, finally, he heard her and slumped—
my father never seemed so puny.
The water stopped and the green-glass
vessel went back to its old dusty niche,
a piece of ceiling later smashed it,
and we resumed living with the bomb.

Hit or Miss

For my twelfth birthday Mom gave me
the bow and arrow set and the straw-stuffed target,
its gold bull's-eye, ringing out to red, blue,
black, white, propped on the green wooden tripod.
These were arrows with aluminum points,
not the broadheads I sometimes found lodged
in backyard trees (poachers' near-deer misses), but
sharp enough: I could bury them breast deep,
up to the fletching, re-collect the six
arrows, then shoot another perfect end.

I take my stance, slowly nock, then draw full,
aim the mark, my lips kissing the bowstring,
hold steady while not breathing, then release—
handshock, *whir* of arrow, blur of feather,
loud canvas *thwock* and the quivering nock—
willing six slight arcs into a tight cluster,
all gold. I imagine loosing myself
in flight, homing toward that certain zone,
Robin-Hooding the previous arrow,
my tip skewering the shaft, dead center.

In time a kind of profound mastery came
and boredom. I'd plink about the backwoods
at whatever struck my fancy—a leaf,
forked twig, old bird's nest—but best was shooting
straight up, losing sight, counting six seconds …
it hurtles back at me, the sound it sings
as it rings into ground. The strike pattern
hugs me, this spot I shoot at, and the air
parries every arrow. My strong right eye
fixes each free fall with a wide black taunt.

Now I Lay Him Down to Sleep

I tuck him gently in his bed tonight
calm his raging against the dying day.
He asks me to stay and leave on the light.

He'd rampaged the house, looking for the right
way out, lathered in sweat, kicking as they,
his caregivers, hid behind armchairs all night.

On my visits home, he gives a fierce bright
smile like sunshine through the landing's grand bay,
he asks me to stay and leave on the light.

He knows something's wrong, is scared into flight,
I tell him straight what is coming his way.
I tuck him gently in his bed tonight,

he says, "You're the Daddy now," as my sight
blears in tears, remembering him as the gray
impresario strutting the footlights.

And you, Dad, so fallen from my heart's height,
once damned me as a boy who would not pray.
I tuck you gently in your bed tonight,
you ask me to stay and leave on the light.

In Dreams Begin Reproaches ...

that wrenching ache when suddenly
I remember what I shouldn't have
forgotten   that Mother was dying
  awed by that lapse's enormity
at how fundamentally broken
I was   a stranger   then the anger
raging   ravaging   raw
and as quick my quenching sorrow
desperate to make amends somehow.
But where is she? Where did I leave her?
as I lurch through the clacking old train
  car after empty car   wondering where
      grasping any improbable clue
arguing still with my failed self
how had I not been and was not there now?
so clear   so clear   that much I owed her
utterly unworthy of my birth
and then   at the last moment I slid
the door open to the room where I
  knew she had just died   even then gone
flowers beside the newly made bed
a note in her neat hand thanked someone
for the last cleaning up with some cash
and on the bed in clear plastic wrap
a furled purple umbrella   *So her*
I immediately thought after
  thinking the opposite   like I did not
know her at all   nor now ever could.
  The train rumbles on and I
thoroughly corrupt   take the money

Father's Day

David, There's Still Time to Show Dad
You Love Him—36% Off from ProFlowers!
                              —email solicitation

I am not sure the language of flowers will
reach him who has been pushing up daisies
for nigh two decades, so Monday I will send him
virtual flowers in my dreams—he would
appreciate my inherited Scottish thrift:
perhaps a bouquet of thyme and rue.

The Attic

I'm a bit verklempt at this needful
closure—I've not quite anticipated it well
even though I knew years ago it was coming—
not in waves but pangs. It's cold and rainy
this All Souls' Day as I go through them that
authored me: the long-boxed papers, travel
itineraries, clippings, date books, drivers' licenses,
passports, canceled checks, diaries, photographs—
we three together once in a yellowed candid.

The delving is the next phase when the heart
of what I will keep can be filed, the rest
tossed. I knew casting back would have a cost,
but I still hope for dividends, too, a few
generous moments of reflection, even
forgiveness. The residue of our lives heaps
up, we defer the sorting out to them
who remain. I hope to leave a tidier footprint,
but if not—here is my apology.

Night

Now I Lay Me

Now, and again, I enjoy the even
breathing of the world, largely it comes at
night when traffic has died down, a car
Dopplers away, molecules sigh, vie
their vibration against the larger register.

I prefer this inward tempest of minuscule
sound even if only in my head this while
to be so attuned when much else is still
in this cocooned moment—BEING—echo
of my heartbeat in the drawing-down night.

Dreamtiger

—*for Jorge Luis Borges*

The tiger ripples
down narrow corridors
of the labyrinth
with no center
the way algebra
conceives or a verb
conjugates itself

black rain lashes
his flaming flexure

each paw print pools
a tiny tiger
in a maze of fire

The Insomniac Scientist Counts Similes

like gathering the googolplex
of beads of mercury floating
in a dark weightless chamber

like solving the Pythagorean theorem
with bread crumbs (SHOW ALL WORK!)

like trying to play tic-tac-toe
on a twisting Rubik's Cube

like memorizing the series of tiny
zeros and ones of the binary code
on a vast Möbius strip in Braille

like sequencing the DNA helix
with Post-its and toothpicks

like waiting hour upon hour
in the hourglass-turned-Klein-bottle
neither inside nor outside the glass

Soundings

I harken to my heart often when here
at rest and ready for descent into sleep,
monitor its steady beat upon beat pulling
me under the mantle of consciousness,
only a matter of time to yet divine
what dwells down there in my benthic murk,
to wrest up salvage from the wreck I am,
diving again, and again, for fractal clues,
mere shards of something never once whole,
debris field scattered over ocean floor
of that irretrievable realm of dream,
willing lucid recovery from shadows
with this diving helmet and feeble torch,
sinking beneath the liminal....

Personae

Dowsing for the Mole at Age Eight

For three days I have allowed the mole
to augment his byzantine dominion.
I have borrowed the kitchen knife
and knotted it to the hazel branch
with twine: a proper dowser
with which to witch the varmint out.

The serrated blade ruptures the black
galleries of his blind scuttle;
he rustles the tunnel with retreat,
loses me at the labyrinth hub.
He urges me over the moled quarter acre
of the front lawn—his meandering mine.
His old ways become caved in, stomped down.

Soon there is only the long corridor—
balked at both ends. He shuttles back
and forth between those walls
that stalk and turn him back again,
that four-foot artery that is his last
precinct of instinct. I steady
my heartbeat, take my time.

Abruptly, he finds his ambit halved.
I am coiled at the midpoint, timing
his dartles. The branch trembles;
then my hand is pulled down sharp
by that mammal's tiny, frantic heart.

Late Summer Afternoon at Pancake Falls

It's a hot day. I enter the cool shallows,
steady my way up to the rapids, turn and sit
in its force, then pull and kick my way
under the cowl of water, within the spillway
where no outside sound can intrude, I abide
within the downpour of my sanctum roar
for what seems an hour, declaiming, laughing.

When I crown out and the sound resounds
in its old way, I urge my sweetheart, who is charcoal
sketching, sitting upon a pancake stone, to
assume the throne under the cascade, which she does.
Monarchs flit about as tawny-orange and
black-veined-stained-glass petals and I collect
them in flight, gently hinging each closed, fore wingtip
to fore wingtip, one after another, then cup them
within my caged fingers—I wait for her.

She emerges from the waterfall, whips her blonde
hair back in a geyser, and falls to the towel
beside me, giddy to tell of her wonderment. I defer
her with the *Voilà* of my open hands—and in
that moment a dozen monarchs startle forth,
beat their wings, flourish a bouquet mirroring
in her pupils. Our laughter drowns the water's fall.

Twenty-one Curves

Hadn't been driving this stretch of road
for a while, lonely route, no other
hurtling vehicles—like that oncoming
in the night fog two years ago that stripped
the chrome with a *thwack*—but fast again
like he used to, racing toward the dead-man's
curve he'd hard-braked through so many
times before, the hairpin one. He knew
the road by rote, hugging the outside,
straying over center for slingshot speed,
braking and gunning alternately through,
counting down each curve, headlights fleeting
off the ditch and trees, through the straightaways
with radio off, windows down, cold, listening
to the peels and skids, juddering in the car
like a ride in a fun park, clenching the wheel
between spins and reverse spins, ticking
them off like years, skins shed, *little molts
left by the side of the road,* he mused. Then
bearing down through the last few to that one
where caution was utmost important—last
straightaway before the torquing turn
readying for it by speeding up—then orange
caution cones and the workmen's barricade
smash through onto bare ground, lurching
on the jerky terrain and the instinctive switch
from gas to brake in the hard rut that was no
longer paved, washed out from the latest flood.
He plowed around the bend, coming at last
to the other barricade, snaking around one end,
regaining the road, slowly, picking up speed.
Never to return to this stretch like he wouldn't
drive down her street after the breakup—solemn
pact—perhaps after all the years she still lives there,
but he wasn't going to drive by now to see.

29

Whether to Laugh or Cry

I see your blonde hair in the theater
emblem of first magnitude, prime mover,
more to it than meets sight for my sore eyes,
where have you been all my lives?
I see hills in your blue sweater:
I'm old as your father and know better
but would give my back teeth to be younger,
my sauce good for us, both goose and gander.
I'm victim of your small, tender mercies
imagined in my pre-midlife crises,
but my old cold feet, your young cold shoulder,
our frozen good turns deserve each other.

A Service Performed

I found the ground outside the high-rise
fourteen flights from the balcony's plumb
a step beyond the railing to here
in that terminal rush of free fall
where on Monday a doubter confirmed
that thirty-two feet per second squared
still was gravity's norm, a body
not yet at rest in the morgue's steel drawer.
I lie down in the spread-eagled die
stamped hard in the flat and browning grass—
her last but not lasting impression—
head, torso, arms, legs cram the hollow,
an eerie custom-fit, I huddle deep into
her last thoughts   *there   there   shhh* ...

For Good Measure

From vantage point to vanishing point
yetta to decca to nano to yacto
spark arcing across synapses
constant of light in one second's flight

high-wire net under the taut lyric line
one head plus six others equal a body's height
how cesium seconds fractionate time
span and cubit, foot and ambit, Scoville scale,

decibel, Richter, altimeter, calorie,
stem to stern, head to toe, from the summit
of ambition to despair's deep-sonar nadir
thirty-two feet per second per second

golden mean, Pythagorean, Euclidean,
A to zed then onto the extended units,
jogging along the Möbius Strip Mall.
Yesterdays roved by a tensile memory

four legs, then two, then three, then none
length, width, depth, time plus n variable dimensions
reentrant knight's tour on its 8^2
resonant frequency's threshold of sorrow,

epicycles and music of the spheres
celesta, theremin, didgeridoo, and viola d'amore,
reductio ad absurdum: binary one and naught,
hash marks on the highway blurring to a solid white line,

g-force traveler in a Coney Island cyclotron
aka The Kelvin Mansion on Lagrangian Point.

Vivarium

You awake to the same crowd all around
a day like every other day so far

nestled in orchid bark while on the glass
the blue morph anole waits for the morning

misting to lap droplets off the pothos
vine, later the shakeout of young, powdered

crickets rich in nutrients, a flying gecko
basks on driftwood below the electric

sun, and a spring peeper croaks a complaint
as you shake off chameleon dreams

of salamandrine fire, and the basilisk
in the corner one-eyes the blue-tongued skink.

You blend into the glass and just wait—
soon that small dark-mottled anole

will lie in the freezer with his maggots,
his cold blood slowed to a stop.

Why Holiday Away?

I will shelter in place for my staycation,
save a bundle without Priceline,
and locovore in my refrigerator,
I have pre-Y2K turkeys in the freezer
and rice and beans to keep my pulse going,
sardines, tuna, nuts, peanut butter, MREs,
and tap water—no exotic bottled H$_2$O.
I've set the house alarm and canceled
the paper delivery, put the lights on a timer
and told the neighbors I will be away.
Why roam abroad when I've done Rome at home!

I will monitor the flight tracker on my
progress—such a smooth ride, tilted back
in my Barcalounger while eyeing in-flight
entertainment on my large screen and no
puling infant, puking passenger, or double-
wide neighbor—I do miss the stewardesses.

It is as if I never left home or packed a bag
or have to worry about liquid allowances or
carry-on fees. No oxygen masks dropping,
no looking for the neon strip while panicking
toward the exit door and the evacuation slide,
no infuriating inundation of in-flight ads
and no duty-free extortion. So, I have laid
in a few mini bottles and large bags of chips
for my less than five-hour-forty-minute soar.

My pockets are full of Swiss Army knives, keys,
change, magnets; there are matches in my shoes,
but my underwear is clean, my belt buckle has C-4
inscribed on it, my first move in online chess.
I take selfies in different rooms, allow the mail
to pile up inside the slot, cross the days off the calendar

till welcome return to home and to work. I rehearse
the narrative of my fantastic holiday, embellish
it in the dark before the mirror. I chose Iceland
this time—so no tan and I'll lose some weight
and my colleagues will comment on how relaxed
I look. I will be heartily welcomed back—all
their illusions preserved—and my pocketful
of krónur miraculously untouched.
I eagerly await the postcards I sent home
to discover what a great time I had while away.
I cross off the days to my next foreign adventure....

Ungently Used

At the tag sale everyone wears
an AS IS nameplate, as it should be:
some are broken with faint cracks,
others dinged about a bit, worn
round the edges, sitting in the corner
not courting notice, or freshly glued,
polished, placed in the sunlight
to best vantage, or jumbled
with others with little prospect,
waiting for a browser to claim them,
someone who doesn't look too closely,
or who does and knows true value,
someone, not merely a collector,
who wants to mend with them,
damaged goods, but good enough.

How do you repair

a pair of socks when one goes missing,
a pair of gloves when one gauntlet lies there
alone by mishap on the sidewalk grate
as its mate grieves elsewhere, and footwear where
one waits for the other one to drop,
a pair of crutches, now hobbling solo?

It's not backgammon with a roll of the die,
two monocles do not eyeglasses make,
it's chic to wear a single earring, or
a chopstick in your updo, not so much one
cuff link or a single ice skate, but some things
are, or should be, inseparable like a pair
of underwear, scissors, handcuffs, jeans.

We all like bilateral symmetry:
I have a pair of eyes, arms, legs, kidneys,
lungs, gonads, and hands—in poker
two pair is not a bad hand. A couple,
a mated pair—one wonders if Noah
sexed his pairs wrong and how many species
went extinct—can go lacking when one
or the other is no longer around.

I like my pairings conjoined like twins or
that string that snakes sleeves to leash mittens
when we were kids, a connection
like the line between those then devices
that were tin cans we walkie-talkied into.

Maybe to avoid despair we need to
always have a spare—sometimes two—a prayer
against that rare nightmare that's hard to bear
when we err in not taking proper care.

Ledgering

Palimpsest

Blind in the dark and mute with pen again,
fingertip parsing the rough paper pad
I know is yellow on a brown clipboard,
along these thin blue latitudes I tack
ink black and forth across my unmapped world,
sole discoverer, maybe not till well after
tomorrow, to decipher what the hooks
on those long lines, the net of their weaving,
what small word-hoard raised from memory's hulk
from that oracular deep where I sleep,
interior of my mother's lone child
hauling my way through the long night I flow,
seeds from my nib's groove sail on sinuous
riverruns, dark sea bleeding out of me.

Sensitive Deep-Sea Fishing

Anticipating in the fighting chair
I am a question mark with one hook as
the weighted barb lowers its lure deeper,
letting out the long line as far as it goes,
waiting patiently (what else?) for …

> *With my cast line finely tuned and set deep,*
> *bait drifting along the benthic zone, angling*
> *for a strike in the perpetual dark*
> *of the abyssal abode of those denizens*
> *deep down, so secretive in the pitch of black*
> *you'd never know they're there unless you catch*
> *one unaware or they want you to know.*

                                    … the nibble
or that strike and run, waiting for that hit
then the slow, hard reeling in, playing out,
redoubled reeling, the rising—that breaking
surface of what had never seen light before,
out of its element and now in mine,
wonderment at what is on the end of the line.

Amanuensis of Anamnesis

My dailiness in flesh made word is not
for posterity's ears. I would write
on the fly if it would promptly die, speck
on the patient paper, in the commonplace
book on the night table where
nothing never happens ad hoc.

My febrile, feeble effort against loss,
with lyrical effusion and musing
on the charades of everyday hours,
one damn thing after another,
every day a new entry and a signing off,

a long, periodic sentence of *vox clamans*
in a stream of resolves and squirreled
details, *aperçus,* and *apologias,*
my millennium of the moment
in a memoir to *memento mori*

to lessen the pain by predicting
the future to make it more bearable
in my steady diet of the first person.
That writing kept for just myself:
a re-collection of recollections,

an oasis of omens, oracles, dreams,
memoranda, poems, the needle's eye
scribbling and sketching nib
in the daily tide of my last writes,
pillow book for my slumbers, opusculum,

a novel with my last chapters ripped out,
an appointment book—*Carpe et cave diem!*

_ _ _ _ _ _ **is:**

three mismatched shoes at the entrance of a dark alley
a dividend from what you know and what you are
an investigation, not an expression, of what you know
a thief that comes in the middle of a new day
deep gossip
a kind of leaving notes for another to find
what makes the invisible appear
a machine for remembering yourself
smuggling of something back from the otherworld
begins and ends in silence
something, rather than just being about something
that to which your being says Yes
a bell that troubles the air long after its sound has stopped
magnificently achieved, or it is negligible
a particular sort of ignorance
much closer to music and mathematics
a fountain
to a large degree sound
diagnostic, rather than therapeutic
between the ears and behind the left nipple
only there to frame the silence
a way of talking to your loved ones when it's too late

Us

Coming

—for Joan

Tonight I walk the dirt road's crown to you
through fat fairy snowflakes, each
white paper lantern glows the way.
It will be an hour more till I nose
the wood smoke from your cabin
that resiny scent I could follow blind.

It's so still even with the muffled crunch
plumes of breaths, blood throb in my ears,
the faint crackle nearby flakes make
as they touch down in the wood.
Twenty minutes more until home …

now there's the slight flicker through the saplings,
your candle gutters in the front window.
I stamp the stoop, open the door, enter.
In a rush you are upon me, dusting off
the snow, pulling off my coat, melting me
with that smile I came for.

Domestic Science

If I were a screwdriver I'd drive-screw
in the evening when handymen are most
handy—not like those daybreak hammermen.
I'd have an adjustable bit and length
for socket heads slotted, crossed, and Phillips'd,
squared, hexed, one-wayed, Bristoled, and French recessed,
engaging my bit with the head, ready
to press hard until set and not cam out—
for none enjoy slipping out of the screw,
inch or metric—then having to reslot,
precision-ratchet the pawl, drive downward,
rotating the shaft in a steady torque,
righty-tightying your star bit till flush
and fully sunk—we both done to a turn.

If

I came back on my shield would you
fall on my sword? Would a stranger
place two piles of three stones each
on the beach where we were last seen?
Would you cut off your right breast
to shoot me through the heart with an arrow?
Would I welcome a sky full of such arrows?
Would we expose our child on a hillside,
foot staked into the ground, until starvation
or fatal mauling by a wild beast? Or
would she take root and wreathe into a laurel?
Will they sing the goat song of our marriage,
how our choruses battled and bristled
between pauses like the summer cicadas
in two lone laurel trees? Then, at night
will the constellations fault themselves?

I want a little boat

with a little bottom
and taut keel to take
a wide sail down
your aboriginal river
banked by wild jungle
your esses yesses
such a certain course …

I want all of you
in the going down of you
bumps and scrapes withal
before the waterfall
to that current place
that is my source

Animalia

Cicadian Rhythm

In the crabapple tree above our
yard, where summer day falls dark,
his lone chirr carries perhaps to
a willing mate flicking her wing,
which he hears and flies toward.

Her eggs hatch and fall
to unencumbered ground,
burrow down in the dark, then
after seventeen nymphal years,
one summer night emerge
from the earth and climb
the same tree their parents
gave them life in, before dying.

Climbing high, claw over claw,
anchor the bark and split
brown armor down the spine,
hunch backs out then broad heads,
lean far into the breeze,
then forward again, clutch
their molt with foreclaws,
and shuck their green selves out

unfurl wet wings to dry
then buzz off imagoes
a few weeks to mate and die.

Soon his black carcass on mown grass,
mealed by moiling ants—
all that might-have-been
life in his strong raspy song

Summer in a Garden State

The breeze near dusk directs the upper branches
of old-world maple trees down the *allée* of our
avenue, each section davens as chorales of courting
cicadas counterpoint *Freude*. Released from
their apprenticed spelunking below suburban sod,
mute these many years, now swan-singing
their last aria of renewed youth at the pinnacle
before begetting then death. Crickets fiddle up
as the cicadas cool down, fireflies yellow,
and in three hours I flashlight the front-yard crabapple
for him, pale malachite cipher Houdini-ing out
his brown old husk, hanging onto it as I, too,
hold fast—true to each new beginning.

Cosmo's Sweet Sixteen

Hunching up his bare-ribbed skeleton
with the tatty, shedding upholstery of fur
against my stroking from neck down toothy
vertebrae to lumbar and still that slight rump-lift
delight, holding in place on shaky legs,

front paws staking out my chest, nuzzling
his familiar chin-on-chin greeting, marking,
then a weak head-butt, finally the clawing up
to inchmeal settle, our wonted cheek to cheek
like how I nursed him with the eyedropper
after that abandonment that still scars him,

and I gently cat-nip an ear tip with my lips,
tug, an intimacy he liked when younger,
or as minikin kitten when his whole
Tootsie Pop head fit into my mouth
then born again into the air he burred loudly.

He scrabbles up onto the headrest, his tail
flicking across my face, then tucks up behind
my head, he is an antimacattar
to my leather Barcalounger, but never

one to wear in a welcome long, he slowly
rises on his pins and labors down
crossing my chest once again, with tail up,
catterdemalion, rumpled in his stilts' skin.

Stormy

The black Lab on his pallet by my bed
is getting older, snout tucked into tail
and hind paws. Not the puppy I slept with
years ago when his people were nearing divorce
and thought he would be good for the family—
a guilty sop to their son—but obedience training
was spotty. Then shuttled from mansion to condo,
insecure, he barks, nips, and sometimes bites.
Electric fences, leashes, muzzles and he's still
not secure in himself as his circumstances
remain uncertain—two months ago he was
nearly taken to a shelter and put down.
But right now, below and beside me, he sleeps,
slightly stretching as I stroke his back.

Blacky

O somnolent poultice here on my lap
licking yourself as I stroke you, humming
your warm lullaby, lulling me to sleep
after kneading my belly with needful
instinct where I am surrogate mother
to your ten-year-old, sixteen-pound black
domestic shorthair self, with third eyelids
veiling green eyes as I knead this palpable loaf
of cat with two-handed massage, taking time
to swipe out crusts in the corners of your eyes,
fingering your gums, chucking chin, teasing
those cool ear-vellum-tufted tips, stroking
cheeks behind the whiskers, then the long
cranial-thoracic-lumbar-sacral-caudal swipe—
against, then with, the grain, and again—
the long ridgeline of vertebrae, deep muscle
rub, scratching that feline chakra at the base
of your rump, which causes you to arch slightly,
raise your tail and burr a bass drone, throbbing
your bulk, and then you quit grooming yourself
and begin licking my fingers fast and furious,
at last settle under my palms, eyes drowse to close;
soon I join you in slumberland—both I suspect
feral in our own creatural natures in dreams—
your warm thrumming on mine and mine on yours

Offsprung

In the next room

The innocent young ladies ululate
separately, then lupine in unison;
our first aggrieved plaintiff enters with all
that fury her four-year-old lungs allow,
few facts are offered in evidence
and the duly noted crocodile tears
don't sway our owlish deliberations—
we, who made her, not born yesterday.

She'd been shoved and now seeks grievous
sanctions against her tormentor. We dismiss
her plea. Next the defendant beelines in,
shrilly presents her vindicatory version
ratcheted up to offset the scales, nullify
any nepotism. We out of hand say NO.

Then her five-year-old sister follows suit,
the self-appointed *neutral* observer
telling tales on everyone, a willing
porcupine before our high kangaroo court.
She belabors jurisparent patience.

Last, the two-year-old lamb bawls her appeal
left out again of the larger circus,
the worst infraction among near equals
because the smallest voice is most ignored.
We soberly render our blind judgment:
all are found out of order, remanded
to *Sleeping Beauty,* popcorn, and new accord.

Almost Six

—for Lauren

I heard her say tonight to her mother
in secret whisper not to tell that she
loves her dad a lot, smile over shoulder,
"No! Don't tell!" as I approach, declaim, "Don't
tell *what?*" in my affected Villain Voice
meant for impish enjoyment as she skirls

and I Frankenstein-forward claws outstretched
gesturing to "tickle spots" under her
armpits: *"NO* Da-ddy!" entreats opposite

replete with giggles and taunts that cast me
in the role of monster and hero,
and I recall her fourth Christmas when I
intoned, "Tiger! Tiger! burning bright—" she
pistoled back, "Won't you guide my sleigh tonight!"

Night Rain

All the houses on our block shine their totems,
welcoming lantern or evil eye, hearth flicker
of TV bluing on the den's ceiling,
perhaps *It's a Wonderful Life* or not.
The sidewalks are quiet, dogs have voided,
the geese honk snow-birding south, another
plane angles its attack toward LaGuardia.

Out by our curb, sodden, is our dead
recently laid out Christmas tree,
Frazier pining away its nineteen years
like the half-dozen others similarly beached,
soon to be chippered down to size, spread
around the trunks of other suburban trees—
but all is not loss, our daughter's smaller tree
shorn of its branches and trimmed to height
leans in our boiler room, a year from now I will
strip off the dried bark for her own walking
staff, to pick out our path in the fall forest.

A wind chime two houses down tolls
delicately in the slight breeze—all families
are happily different or differently happy.

Night Tide

I slip under her covers and snuggle in
and she turns toward me, nestles closer,
begins to put her arm around me
then brings it down to cross her breast, buries
her head into my chest, breathing softly—
I'd not quite call it *snore*—and I stroke her
hair while she continues her disyllable
draw-blow, the inhale a bit raspier—
due to stuffiness and unwillingness
to blow her nose—so that it sounds like
fa-ther ... fa-ther ... fa-ther ... fa-ther ... fa-ther,
a trochee letting me know who I am.

I lie there for minutes listening to her
calling me, naming me, steadily,
almost succumbing to that chantlike rhythm,
drifting further away—*fa-ther ... fa-ther*
calling me back.

Jumble

A shoal of large wooden letters huddled by
the curb on Thirtieth Street near Penn Station
as I passed. There were not many but I turned
back thinking *I might find her there.* Guilty for
my public scavenging I hurriedly tried to piece
unlikely her together with a lowercase *l*, two *a*'s,
one broken, and two *u*'s, one for an upside down
n—but no *e* or *r*. All day at work I fretted
my return to the scene. All was cleared except
for, just off the curb, that lipogram *e*—EUREKA!
When I came home I carved out the broken *a*
into a smaller *r*. I have her in the anagrams
"neural," "unreal"—our "lauren."

Yesterday My Little Girl

Yesterday my little girl phoned me—she
sounded so far away, her voice so small—
and I went on alert because I thought
she was downstairs watching TV. "I am
in our front yard going to sleep with Blacky,
make sure I am not taken…." I get up,
go outside, sit on a corner of blanket
as our cat circles and she sleeps and I read
in the late afternoon light, stroking him
as he patrols, brushing back and forth.
She sleeps face up with a slight snore
while I sit vigil as guardian dad.
I eye slow, passing cars, and Blacky settles
as a large dark front moves in—I delay
this moment for as long as I can, till
those first peltings of rain, then rouse her
sleepy-eyed-self to go inside and wait out
our five-month college-bound countdown.

Leaving Home

Two-and-half-hour drive up to Troy
just the three of us—our nuclear unit—
but only two of us will come back.

Her mother and I watched her check in, get
her photo ID and dorm room key, then
drove over and began unpacking the car,
carrying up the mini fridge, etcetera,
to her third-floor single, turning the bare
furniture and spare layout into a bright
thirteen-by-thirteen-foot temporary home
until May. We had a late afternoon lunch
at Dinosaur BBQ beside the Hudson,
bought some further necessities at ACE Hardware,
then back to the dorm for the final good-byes:
a selfie of we three looking sad—then one happy.

The long mom hug and *I love you*s, then me:
Remember these three things, first: work hard;
second: have responsible fun; third: I love you!

Outside another mom embrace, then me:
We had a long hug, then on a whim I lifted her
off the ground. *See I can still "pik m'up"!*

She chuckled as I set her back down. We turned
to begin our walks away, then I stole a look back
and saw just her back.

Reverie

I awake but do not open my eyes,
let the lingering dream movie play
again, and again. She is lying on me,
her left ear against my heart, arms around
and holding on tight, not ready to let go.

I cradle her in my arms, wondering
how this wonder came to be and I say,
"Sweetie, you seem so small again." And she,
"But, I am, Daddy!" and hugs me tighter.

Amazed and grateful in this vision's wake,
I invoke it to rerun: her embrace
weakens, the color fades to shadow.
Dawn and daylight dispel any vestige
of illusion or solace this uncommon
presence might have left. I lose you again.

Then

Here Lies the Body of My Work

—after E.L.M.

The dirt under my feet dreams of greeting
me. I lay my head beneath the hill
where others are sleeping, still, long after
their warfare on life, under tumbledown
graven headstones in holy ground,
cankerworms' meals. Each of us long unwept for,
quiescent souls abroad in this distant
land, dust of our dust with kindred spirits.

From here under the shadow of elms
rooted as undertenants of the earth
we look over the meadow rue and river—
and abide to be reclaimed.

Per Aspera

Ascend the ash of stairs
through the dark dust of night
to the stars, chandelier of ice.
There is a stair of air to there
that begins with the first step up,
rising higher to the next tread,
a spiral stair for the daring aspirer,
just let loose and lose the earth,
arise higher and higher, climb
each ascent like a wingbeat,
each assent bodying upward.
Now you are the stair—
do not despair in midair—
not the one once hoped for,
long lost, but this sturdier, truer one,
won in the getting to here from there.

Walled In

All was a dead reckoning toward
a room of my own, my last, narrow
house, too small a dwelling to
entertain an echo, waiting for the first
spider, here, where darkness bears its fruit,

and no window tax to pay, just these
daily rounds of lying-in as I keep
my few accounts on one thumbnail,
counting the cats of Zanzibar,
out on the ocean of being alone,
solitude so companionable.

I am relieved that when I came to die
I discovered that I at least had lived.

An Abidance

My dormant bones lie fallow
beneath the alluvial plain,
naked scaffolding caved in,
a bundle of hingeless sticks—
poor résumé of a stilled life.

My crumpled armature, seized
up like a contortionist's,
is a cache of osier rods,
yarrow staves, a collapsed
wigwam with cracked ribs.

My skull is fissured with meridians.
The compass rose squats on my dome
with implacable fixity, pressing me
into Prairie. This bowl is tenanted
by sediment and my seed of memory.

My unstrung vertebrae tingle
when the rattlesnake sidles over—
Oh Great Spirit, let his cord reeve
my rings again. Raise me up in situ!

Publication Acknowledgments

I gratefully thank the editors of the journals and anthologies who accepted the poems found in this collection:

Barrow Street "Civil Defense," (Summer 2002), "Night Rain" (Winter 2008), "Blacky" (Winter 2017)

The Fossil Record "Beachhead" (online, 2014)

Istanbul Literary Review "Whether to Laugh or Cry," "Vivarium" (online, 2009)

The Jefferson Journal "Late Summer Afternoon at Pancake Falls" (Fall 2015)

The Kean Review "In Dreams Begin Reproaches," "Now I Lay Him Down to Sleep," "Almost Six," "Summer in a Garden State" (Fall/Winter 2009)

Lips "A Service Performed" (Fall 2008/Winter 2009)

Love Poems "Coming" (Barnes & Noble anthology, 2002)

Manhattan Literary Review "Coming," "Cicadian Rhythm" (Autumn 2003)

Morning Song: Poems for New Parents "Almost Six" (St. Martin's Press anthology and audiobook, 2011)

Poetry "An Abidance," "Dowsing for the Mole at Age Eight" (December 1990)

The Seventh Quarry "Palimpsest," (Summer 2010), "The Insomniac Scientist Counts Similes" (Summer 2011), "Night Tide" (Spring 2014)

The Stillwater Review "Jumble," "_ _ _ _ _ _ is:" (2013)

Voices From Here 2 (The Paulinskill Poetry Project) "Listen" and "Per Aspera" (2017)

Personal Acknowledgments

After graduating with a history BA from the University of Virginia in 1977, I flirted with a Ph.D. in ancient history, also at UVA, but transferred to the English department, taking poetry writing workshops with Donald Justice, Carolyn Forché, and Gregory Orr, and earning an MA with a concentration in poetry writing in 1981. Then I beelined to the Big Apple to begin my long career in the accidental profession—trade book publishing—which was not that accidental as I knew I wanted to be in publishing after helping to initiate the biannual *Virginia Literary Review* at UVA in 1979. The *VLR* is ongoing and the oldest literary magazine on the Grounds.

After the allure of New York City and "professional" responsibilities paled, I renewed taking poetry writing workshops, in the evenings from various venues in Manhattan and then later also in New Jersey, with a slew of poet/teachers: Laurel Blossom, Nicholas Christopher, Elaine Equi, Brooks Haxton, Richard Howard, Michael Lally, David Lehman, Pearl London, Kathy Ossip, Kevin Pilkington, Martha Rhodes, Hugh Seidman, Rebecca Seiferle, and Karen Swenson. I am grateful for their constructive comments and guidance, as well as the thoughtful and helpful support from my fellow poet/students.

I have to give a shout-out to two mentors. I was privileged to take six workshops over a ten-year span, beginning in the early nineties at New York University, with William Packard— poet, playwright, novelist, and translator. Bill was a daunting physical and mental presence, and a passionate proponent of cutting through the BS and getting to the true emotional core of students' poems. *He cared.* Not long after he died in 2002, I began teaching his poetry workshops at NYU, and that sense of connection carries over when I find myself echoing his precepts to my students. Also, the ground-breaking magazine he began in 1969, *New York Quarterly,* established

78

an imprint in 2009, NYQ Books, which is the publisher of the book you are now holding—another felicitous connection to Bill.

I began taking an advanced poetry writing workshop at The New School with poet and author Patricia Carlin (co-editor of Barrow Street Press) in 2000 and did so for thirty-one semesters, up to her retirement. Patricia is much missed by her Carlinistas—my coinage for the devout following of her students over the years. Patricia has a rigorous intelligence, broad and deep knowledge of all things poetry, and is a champion for poetry in general and for the particular poem under discussion in her workshop. *She cared.* Patricia has read and provided written comments on 605 of my poems—yes, I kept an accounting. Further, she has generously read and given advice on several iterations of the manuscript that eventually morphed into this debut, full-length collection of my poems. All but two of the poems in *Ledger Domain* were written during that thirty-one-semester-long workshop, and I am indebted, also, to Patricia's enthusiastic encouragement to persevere with the manuscript and see it through to publication.

Lastly, for the many of you out there who are also poets—published or not, yet—I would like to share a brief anecdote on how after the many submissions to contests and publishers over the years LEDGER DOMAIN became upper/lowercased and italic. I wrote a review for *American Book Review,* and asked Barry Wallenstein, my editor there and a well-known poet/educator, to read the manuscript, which he did, and then suggested I submit it to Raymond Hammond, who took over the *New York Quarterly* magazine at Packard's request before his death. At Raymond's helmsmanship the book publishing imprint flourished, which has given its roster of poets a much-appreciated venue for their voices to be heard and to endure.

79

In late June, 2018, I sent an email query to Raymond; he replied that evening, saying he would read the manuscript, which I sent the next morning, then two and a half hours later: "Just sat down for a minute between killing weeds and going into the office. Read the first two poems—very nice. So, unless there is some hidden poem in the collection that changes my mind, it looks like we will be working on a book together."

Notes

Ledger Domain contains—I hope—a bit of legerdemain to which the gentle reader will not be averse.

"Now I Lay Him Down to Sleep," is a villanelle that uses borrowed terminal words with one substitution end rhyme from Dylan Thomas's villanelle "Do not go gentle into that good night."

"Whether to Laugh or Cry" borrowed clichés from *Clichés: Over 1500 Phrases Explored and Explained* by Betty Kirkpatrick.

"Amanuensis of Anamnesis" borrowed terms and phrases from Thomas Mallon's *A Book of One's Own: People and Their Diaries.*

"_ _ _ _ _ is:" borrowed twenty-two "definitions" of poetry from *The Bloodaxe Book of Poetry Quotations,* edited by Dennis O'Driscoll. The definitions, in order, are from: Charles Simic, Czesław Miłosz, Mark Doty, James Liddy, Liam Rector, Matthew Hollis, Nathalie Sarraute, Don Paterson, Nuala Ni Dhomhnaill, Edward Hirsch, Reginald Shepherd, Seamus Heaney, Christian Wiman, Dana Gioia, Jaan Kaplinski, Margaret Atwood, Michael Longley, Nuala Ni Dhomhnaill, Alica Ostriker, Douglas Dunn, Alice Oswald, and Ted Hughes.

"Here Lies the Body of My Work" derives its tone and some borrowed words from Edgar Lee Masters's *Spoon River Anthology.*

"Walled In" borrowed words and phrases from Henry David Thoreau's *Walden; or, Life in the Woods.*

photo by Lauren Burr

David Stanford Burr is a publishing professional with thirty-seven years of experience in book publishing, currently at St. Martin's/Macmillan and serving as managing editor for trade paperback books. He earned a certificate in Book Publishing from New York University and is an adjunct associate professor, currently teaching a poetry workshop in NYU's School of Professional Development, Center for Advanced Liberal Arts. He was a member of the Advisory Board for *The Chicago Manual of Style* (fifteenth edition).

As editor, David prepared seven hardcover poetry anthologies that remain in print, and he is the author of *The Poet's Notebook: Inspiration, Techniques, and Advice on Craft.*

David is a freelance copyeditor of poetry manuscripts (currently totaling 280 titles) for major New York City trade book publishers. He has copyedited the last dozen *Best American Poetry* annuals.

His chapbook, DAUGHTER, is seeking a publisher, and he is at work on a full-length collection of his own World War I poems, from the bleak perspective of the British infantry in the trenches on the Western Front.

He served for four years as president of South Mountain Poets, which meets in Short Hills, New Jersey, and remains an active participant. He lives in Maplewood, New Jersey, with his wife and their daughter, when she is home from college.

CPSIA information can be obtained
at www.ICGtesting.com
Printed in the USA
FFHW020827051119
55952454-61785FF